Excel Formulas And Functions

Cool Tips and Tricks With Formulas in Excel

Table Of Contents

Synopsis

Microsoft Excel, developed by Microsoft, is a spreadsheet that can run on Windows, macOS, Android and iOS. It features calculation, graphing tools, pivot tables and a microprogramming language known as the Visual Basic for Applications, thereby enabling it to perform complex calculations and data analysis through the usage of formulas and functions. Excel has a wide range of applications being popularly used in public finance offices, or any office dealing with accounting. The use of Excel formulas, functions, tools and various operations not only cut the time used in performing data analyses, but also creates outputs, i.e. information that can easily be understood, more dynamic and engaging to stakeholders. This book uses simple understandable language to explore the formula and functions that are useful for computing and managing data. By reading this book, you will learn about mathematical functions, statistical functions, conditional calculations and lookup tables with added cool tricks to enhance your workability.

Note: Functions and tools used in this book relate to Microsoft Excel 2016 and may slightly vary from other previous versions of MS Excel, such as the 2010 and 2013 versions.

Chapter One: Introduction

Short History of Excel

In 1982, Microsoft developed and released a spreadsheet program known as Multiplan which gained popularity on CP/M systems. Multiplan quickly lost its popularity on MS-DOS systems to Lotus 1-2-3, prompting Microsoft to develop a new electronic spreadsheet termed as Excel by enhancing every feature on the Lotus 1-2-3. By 1988, Excel outsold Lotus 1-2-3, increasing the popularity of Microsoft as the top software developer. Through regular releases after every two years or more i.e.1985, 1987, 1990, 1992, 1993, 1995, 1997, 1999, 2000, 2001, 2003, 2007, 2010, 2013 and 2016, Microsoft proved its dominance in the software development sector. The latest release, Excel 2016 (v16.0) as part of Microsoft Office 2016, has new enhanced features, developed to enable users to perform data analysis and interpretation through the following new tools which we will discuss later in detail:

- Excel forecasting functions

- Read-only mode for Excel

- Power query integration

- New graphically-enhanced data charts

- Excel forecasting functions

- Time grouping and Pivot Chart Drill Down

- Excel data cards

- Quick data linking in Visio

- Support for a multi-selection of slicer items using touch

How do Microsoft Excel Function?

Microsoft Excel is actually a form of programming supported through Microsoft's Visual Basic for Applications (VBA), which is a form of Visual Basic Programming. This kind of visual basic programming allows spreadsheets to be manipulated in a unique manner not possible with standard spreadsheet techniques. Excel users basically write codes directly through the use of Visual Basic Editor (VBE) which provides a window for writing code, debugging code, and code module organization environment through the use of data. An Excel Object Model is essential for the VBA code to interact with the spreadsheet objects through a use of unique functions that enable a user to read and write the virtual spreadsheet. The action of imputing and analyzing data is regulated and is executed by the user-created VBA subroutines which operate like macros generated using the macro recorder.

Chapter Two: Microsoft Excel 2016 Layout and Features

The Microsoft Excel 2016 is slightly different from its predecessor version (MS-Excel 2013) as Microsoft always includes new features to a new product, attempting to make the product more useful or correcting mistakes in the previous version. One of the most noticeable features in Excel 2016 is the enhanced Microsoft Power BI compatibility. This feature enables users to publish their Excel workbooks right to their Power BI site, creating highly interactive reports and dashboards based on the user's workbook data. This feature also enables real-time data sharing with other organizations, increasing data efficiency. Apart from the Power BI site, all other features appear similar without much difference. If you were using Excel 2013, you will certainly easily understand the workability of MS-Excel 2016.

Excel 2016 Screen Layout

On opening the Excel worksheet, a window is automatically displayed on the screen as an avenue for you to interact with the software by typing data into the window. The window resembles the one below.

A *Quick Access Toolbar*: It is located on the upper-left corner of the window. Its function is to provide commands used frequently such as Save, Undo, and Redo which appear on the toolbar by default. The Save function saves your file, Undo refutes an action and Redo cancels the Undo function.

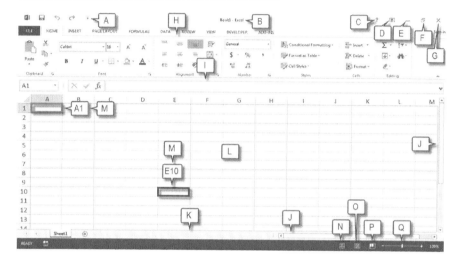

B. **Title Bar**: Located in the top center of the window right to the Quick Access toolbar. It displays the title of the workbook displayed. The first workbook is usually named Book 1 with other workbooks named sequentially from the first worksheet.

C. **Help Button**: Located on the upper-right corner of the window, the Help button enables you to search Excel for information on how you can perform a certain function or formulae.

D. **Ribbon Display Options Button**: It is found right next to the Help Button. You can use it to choose how to display the Excel Ribbon, i.e. Auto-hide Ribbon, Show Tabs, and Show Tabs and Commands.

E. *Minimize Button*: It is located next to the Ribbon Display Options button and it is used to remove the Excel window from view minimizing it to an icon on the Task Bar. You can restore the Excel icon on the Task Bar to restore the Excel window.

F. *Restore Down Button*: It's just right next to the Minimize Button and can be used to reduce the size of the Excel Window.

G. *Maximize Button*: It is used to extend the Excel window to fill the computer's screen. On clicking the Maximize button, it automatically turns into the Restore Down button.

H. *Close Button*: Located on the far end of the window with its main function being closing active workbooks. If the workbook is not saved, a dialogue box opens asking you to save the work done before closing. The Close button also shuts down the Excel software.

I. *Ribbon*: The Ribbon located on the Title Bar can be used to issue commands.

J. *Formula Bar*: The Formula bar can optionally be found below the Ribbon. It is used in entering and editing data. You can display your Formula Bar through the following steps:

1. Choose the View tab.

2. Click the Formula Bar in the Show group. Excel displays the Formula Bar.

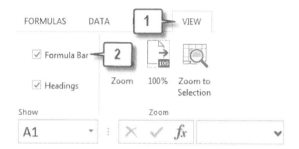

K. *Horizontal and Vertical Scroll Bars*: Both bars can be the contents in the window up, down and across by dragging the icon located on a scroll bar. The vertical scroll bar is located along the right side of the window, while the horizontal scroll bar is just above the Status bar. To your window up and down, you click and drag the vertical scroll bar and, to move back and forth across your workbook, click and drag the icon on the horizontal scroll bar back and forth.

L. *Status Bar*: It appears at the very bottom of the window and provides information, such as the sum, the average, and the count of selected numbers. By right-clicking the Status bar and selecting the options you prefer from the Customize Status menu, you have the option to change what displays on the Status bar.

M. *Worksheet:* It is the actual location where you input your data. Each worksheet is made up of columns and rows. Columns are lettered from A to Z, while the rows are numbered from 1 to infinite depending on the amount of data and can only be limited by the computer's memory.

N. *Cells*: The worksheet is divided into cells. A cell address is a combination of column co-ordinates and a row co-ordinate making up a cell address. A cell is identified through their cell addresses. For instance, a cell located on the upper left corner of a worksheet a called cell A1, indicating it is found between column A and row 1.

O. **Normal Button**: Its function is to format the worksheet for easy data entry.

P. **Page Layout Button**: Important when you need to print your workbook by displaying your workbook, making it easy for you to choose the most appropriate printing option.

Q. **Zoom Slider and Zoom**: The Zoom slider enables you to zoom in and out of your workbook. You can zoom out by dragging the slider to the left and zoom in by dragging the slider to the right. If the zoom slider is selected on the Status bar menu, it appears on the Status bar with the percentage of zoom appearing to the right of the Zoom slider.

Navigating in the Excel Environment

The following keyboard keys are useful in navigating the Excel Environment.

Key	Descriptions
ARROW KEYS	Moves one cell up, down, left or right in a worksheet. SHIFT+ARROW KEY extends the selection of cell by one cell.
BACKSPACE	Deletes one character to the left of the Formula Bar. It also clears the content of the active cell. In cell editing mode, it deletes the character to the left of the insertion point.
DELETE	It removes cell contents (data and formulas) from selected cells without affecting cell formats or comments. In cell editing mode, it deletes the character to the right of the insertion point.

END	Moves to the cell in the lower right corner of the window when
	SCROLL LOCK is turned on.
	Also selects the last command on the menu when a menu or submenu is visible.
	CTRL+END moves to the last cell on a worksheet, in the lowest
	used row of the rightmost used column. If the cursor is in the formula bar, CTRL+END moves the cursor to the end of the text.
	CTRL+SHIFT+END extends the selection of cells to the last used cell on the worksheet (lower right corner). If the cursor is in the
	formula bar, CTRL+SHIFT+END selects all text in the formula bar from the cursor position to the end – this does not affect the
	height of the formula bar.
ENTER	Completes a cell entry from the cell or the Formula Bar, and selects the cell below (by default).

ESC	Cancels an entry in the cell or Formula Bar. Closes an open menu or submenu, dialog box, or message window.
HOME	Moves to the beginning of a row in a worksheet. CTRL+HOME moves to the beginning of a worksheet.
PAGE DOWN	Moves one screen down in a worksheet.
PAGE UP	Moves one screen up in a worksheet.
SPACEBAR	In a dialog box, performs the action for the selected button, or selects or clears a check box. CTRL+SPACEBAR selects an entire column in a worksheet. SHIFT+SPACEBAR selects an entire row in a worksheet. CTRL+SHIFT+SPACEBAR selects the entire worksheet.

TAB	Moves one cell to the right in a worksheet.

Chapter Three: Working with Microsoft Excel 2016

Creating Workbooks from Scratch

There are three ways in which you can create workbooks. First, you can open a new, blank workbook on launching Excel, or by accessing the Backstage through the File tab. Secondly, you can open an existing Excel workbook and enter new or additional data and later save the workbook with a unique name under a different folder. A template can also be used to create a new workbook. It is easier to create a customized workbook through the use of a Template as it has already been set up to display certain kinds of data, such as reports, invoices and so on.

Creating a Workbook from Scratch

A workbook is created from scratch by launching Excel and selecting a blank workbook or another type of template. To launch a new Excel workbook, first click the File Tab, then click New followed by clicking a Blank workbook.

Steps in Creating a Workbook from Scratch

1. Click **BLANK WORKBOOK**. A blank workbook opens with A1 as the active cell.

2. You can type the title of the workbook on cell A1. The text appears both in the cell and in the formula bar.

3. After you've finished typing, press **ENTER**. The text will be entered into cell A1.

4. In cell A2, type the title of the column and press **ENTER**.

5. To open a second workbook, click **BLANK WORKBOOK** in the Backstage view. A second Excel window will open and Book 2 appears in the title bar.

Saving Workbooks

An Excel file can be saved in a folder on your computer's hard drive, a network drive, disc, CD, USB drive, OneDrive or other storage locations. It's up to you to decide where you would want to save the file as the save process is the same in all the storage locations. The default storage location in MS-Excel is the Document Folder or on the OneDrive, depending on settings specified during the program installation.

Steps in Naming and Saving a Workbook.

1. Click the **FILE** tab to open the Backstage view. In the left pane, click Save As to display the save options.

2. Double-click **THIS PC** to open Save As the dialog box.

3. In the navigation pane on the left, in the Save As dialog box, click **DESKTOP**. The Desktop becomes the new file destination of your saved file.

4. In the Save As dialog box, click **NEW FOLDER**. A folder icon appears and you can name it.

5. Type the name of the file and then press **ENTER.**

6. Finally, click the **SAVE** button to save your workbook.

Saving Excel Files to Your OneDrive

OneDrive is a cloud-based application which allows users to store and sync files to the application's database, enabling them to access the files from anywhere on any device with an option of sharing the files with other users. Back-up files of important documents can also be stored on the application.

Steps in Saving Files to Your OneDrive

1. Click the **FILE** tab and then click **SAVE AS**.

2. In the Backstage view, under Save As, click your **ONEDRIVE** account, and then click a folder location in the right pane. You must have a OneDrive account to save files.

3. Click the **NEW FOLDER** button in the Save As dialog box.

4. Type the name of the file in the New folder text box and then press **ENTER** to save to your OneDrive.

Saving in Different File Formats

In Excel 2016, files can be saved in other formats other than .xlsx or .xls. The file formats are listed as options in the Save As dialog box or on the Export tab depending on what type of file format the application supports. It is important to note that when you save data in another file format, some of the formatting, data and features might be lost.

Steps in Saving Files in Different File Formats

You should use a previously saved file.

1. Click the **FILE** tab, and then click the **EXPORT** button.

2. Click the **CHANGE FILE TYPE** button.

3. Click the **CREATE PDF/XPS DOCUMENT** option.

4. In the right pane, click the **CREATE PDF/XPS** button.

5. In the left navigation pane, click **DESKTOP**.

6. Double-click the file you would want to change the format and move it to that folder.

7. In the Publish as PDF or XPS dialog box, ensure that the Save As type list shows PDF.

8. Then, click **PUBLISH.**

9. The reader application (or a Web browser) opens with the PDF file displayed.

10. Press **ALT+F4** to close the browser or Reader application.

11. If necessary, press **ALT + TAB** to return to the Excel file.

Entering and Editing Basic Data in a Worksheet

Basically, data is entered into a worksheet cell through typing. You can also copy and paste information from another worksheet or from other programs. You should make sure that the desired cell for data input is always active by placing the cursor on it. The tab key is used to move to the next column after text is entered.

Entering Data in a Worksheet

As stated above, data is entered through typing. When you finish typing entries in a row, press Enter to move to the beginning of the next row. You can also use the arrow keys to move to an adjacent cell, or click on any cell to make that cell active.

Steps in Entering Basic Data in a Worksheet - Practical Example

1. Click cell **A1**, type International Cop, and then press **ENTER**. The whole active cell should move to the next row.

2. In cell A2, type stuff list and then press **ENTER.**

3. Click cell **A4**, type **NAME**, and then press **TAB**. The active cell moves to the next column, to cell B4.

4. Type Department and then press **ENTER.**

5. Type Lincoln Williams and then press **TAB.**

6. Type Accounting and then press **ENTER.**

7. Type Jefferson Michaels and then press **TAB.**

8. Type Procurement and then press **ENTER.**

This is just an example of entering basic data in a worksheet and you may use your own personal data for practice. Take note that the text is stored in only one cell, even when it appears to extend to the adjacent cells. If a data entry is longer than the cell width and the next cells contain data, the entry appears in a truncated form.

Changing the Column Width

The column width in Excel is established based on existing data. It is necessary to adjust the column width when you add an entry in a column that extends beyond the column's width in order to accommodate the entry. Below are steps in changing a column width manually:

1. Move the mouse pointer between columns A and B in a workbook. The mouse pointer changes to a double-headed arrow.

2. Double-click the column marker between A and B. The width of the column changes to the widest entry in column A.

3. Drag the double-headed arrow mouse pointer between columns B and C until the ScreenTip shows Width: 20 (145 pixels) or a number close to this figure. After dragging the double-headed arrow mouse pointer, release the mouse button to change the column width.

4. Save your workbook.

Editing a Cell's Contents

One advantage of MS-Excel over manual workbooks is that you can easily change the contents of a cell without having to interfere with the whole workbook. To edit information in a worksheet, you can make changes directly in a cell or edit the contents of a cell in the formula bar, located between the ribbon and the worksheet. You should have noted that when you enter data in a cell, the text or numbers appear in the cell and in the formula bar. You can also enter data directly in the formula bar. Before changes can be made, however, you must select the information that is to be changed. Selecting text refers to highlighting the text that is to be changed. You can select a single cell or a portion of the cell's text in the formula bar before you make changes. You can also double-click in a cell to position the insertion point for editing.

Deleting and Clearing a Cell's Contents

To erase the entire contents of a cell, click the cell and then press Delete. This deletes what is in the cell rather than the cell itself. To erase the contents of more than one cell, select all the cells that you want to erase and, on your keyboard, press Delete. Pressing Delete removes the cell's contents, but does not remove any formatting (such as bold, italic, or a different number format) that you may have applied to the cell.

Using Data Types to Populate a Worksheet.

Three types of data can be entered in Excel - namely texts, numbers and formulas. Common data types such as dates can be entered through the use of Auto Fill to complete data in a series. The Flash Fill can also be used to speed data entry down a column. Working with Excel demands that you input accurate data as Excel only calculates and analyzes data based on the numeric values you enter. Of course, if you input wrong numbers, you get wrong calculations, or, rather, inaccurate information.

Entering Dates

Dates are essential in worksheets to track data over a specified period of time. Dates can be used as row and column headings, just like common texts; however, dates are sequential as they are considered as serial numbers and can be added, subtracted and used in calculations. Dates can also be used in formulas as in developing graphs and charts. The way a date is initially displayed in a worksheet cell depends on the format in which you type the characters. Excel 2016 uses four digits for the year as the default date format. Also, the dates are right-justified in the cells.

Steps in Entering Dates

1. Click cell **B5**, type **1/4/2018**, and then press **ENTER.**

2. Click cell **B6,** type **1/25/18**, and then press **ENTER**. The date is entered in B6 as 1/25/2017 and B7 becomes the active cell.

3. Type **1/23** and then press **ENTER**, 23-Jan is entered in the cell. Click cell **B7** and notice that 1/23/20xx (with XX representing the current year) appears in the formula bar.

4. If the year displayed in the formula bar is not 2018, click cell **B7** and then press **F2**. Change the year to **2018** and then press **ENTER.**

5. In cell B8, type **1/28/18** and then press **ENTER.**

6. In cell **B9,** type JANUARY **21, 2018** and then press ENTER. 21-Jan-18 appears in the cell. If you enter a date in a different format than specified or had already entered something in the cell and deleted it, your worksheet might not reflect the results described.

Filling a Series with Auto Fill

The Auto Fill option provided by Excel automatically fills cells with data and/or formatting. To populate a new cell with data that exists in an adjacent cell, use the Auto Fill feature either through the command or the Fill handle. The Fill handle refers to a small green square in the lower right corner of a selected cell or range of cells. A range is a group of adjacent cells that you can select to perform operations on all selected cells. In a range of cells, the first cell and the last cell are separated by a colon e.g. C4:H4.

To use the fill handle, point to the lower right corner of the cell or range until the mouse pointer turns into a +. Click and drag the fill handle from cells that contain data to the cells you would want to fill with that data, or have Excel automatically continue a series of numbers, numbers and text combinations, dates, or time periods, based on an established pattern. To choose an interval for your series, type the first two entries, select them, and then use the fill handle to expand the series of numbers, numbers and text combinations, dates, or time periods, based on an established pattern. To choose an interval for your series, type the first two entries, select them, and then use the fill handle to expand the series using the pattern of the two selected cells.

Steps in Using the Auto Fill Command and Fill Handle to Populate Cells with Data

1. From a previous workbook, select the range C4:H4.

2. On the Home tab in the Editing group, click the Fill button. The Fill menu appears as below:

3. From the menu, click right and the contents of a highlighted cell will be filled into all the cells towards the right.

4. From the workbook, select a range of cells, for instance C9:C13, and then click the Fill button. Choose Down. The content of C9 is copied into the four additional cells.

5. Click on a cell containing months e.g. cell C4, point to the fill handle in the lower right corner of the cell and drag it to E4 and release. The Auto Fill options button appears next to the range, and January through March is displayed.

6. To format data with a common sign such as the dollar sign or commas, click the Auto Fill Options button, and choose Fill Formatting Only from the list that appears. All the numbers are formatted with a common sign.

Filling a Series with Flash Fill

The Flash Fill is another feature that can be used to seamlessly fill data and save time. With Flash Fill, you can quickly fill a column of data using an example that is based on existing data in adjacent columns. Below are steps you can use Flash Fill to quickly fill a column of data.

1. For instance, you have a workbook with a list of customers in column A, which includes the last name followed by a comma and then the first name. You want to create separate columns for the fast and last names.

2. Select cell **B2** in the First Name column.

3. Type **ALVIN** and then press Enter.

4. In cell B3, type **AL** to begin the next first name, Excel guesses the name you would want to enter and would provide Alice as the first suggestion.

5. Press **ENTER** to accept the suggestion; the remaining first names fill down the column. The same applies to the last name column.

Editing a Workbook's Properties

The workbook has a number of properties and features meant to make its management easier. The properties include items that you can indirectly change, such as file size and last edit date. The workbook properties also include items you can directly change such as keywords. Assigning keywords to the documents properties makes it easier to organize and find documents. You can also add more notes to your file for classification and document management.

Assigning Keywords

For instance, if you are working on a workbook containing data about a sales company, you might assign the keyword sales to worksheets that contain data about revenue. You can then search for and locate all files containing information about sales. You can assign more than one keyword to a document. Here are steps in assigning keywords to a document.

1. Click **FILE**. The Backstage view displays current properties on the right side of the window.

2. At the bottom of the right pane, click the **SHOW ALL PROPERTIES** link to display additional properties.

3. Click the **TAGS** field and type **CUSTOMER, SQ FT, PRICE**.

4. Click the **CATEGORIES** field and type **REVENUE.**

5. Click the **COMPANY** field and type the name of the company.

6. Above the Size field, click the **PROPERTIES** drop-down arrow, and then click **ADVANCED PROPERTIES**. The Properties dialog box automatically opens.

7. Click the **SUMMARY** tab in the dialog box to see the properties you entered.

8. Click the **STATISTICS** tab to see the date you modified the file.

9. Click **OK** to close the Properties dialog box.

10. Press **ESC** to return to the worksheet.

11. **SAVE** the workbook in your preferred folder.

After a file is saved, the Statistics tab records when the file was accessed and when it was modified. It also identifies the person who last saved the file. After a workbook is saved, the Properties dialog box title bar displays the workbook name.

Chapter Four: Using Basic Formulas

Formulas are arguably the most powerful feature of Excel enabling it to keep the gold standards over the years. Excel enables you to create many formulas by simply typing in a cell or using your mouse pointer to select cells to include in a formula. For instance, you can create basic formulas for addition, subtraction, multiplication and division using certain methods.

The Difference Between Formulas and Functions

However, it is important to note the difference between formulas and functions in Excel so that you can appropriately use it in your workbooks. Formulas are mathematical equations used to perform calculations in an Excel worksheet or workbook, while functions are predefined formulas that perform calculations in an Excel worksheet or workbook. Both formulas and functions need to be written in a specific way, referred to as syntax, for it to function effectively. Both also need at least one argument; which, on the most basic level, identifies the values for which to perform the action.

- For formulas, the basic syntax is equal (=) function name (AVERAGE, in the example) and an argument. In this case, (A1:A20) is the argument

  =AVERAGE (A1:A20).

- For functions, the basic syntax is equal (=), function name (ROUND, in the example below), argument, and argument tooltip, which is an additional action to perform (2, in the example below represents 2 digits)

=ROUND (A1,2)

Understanding and Displaying Formulas

On clicking on Formulas Tab on the Excel Ribbon, the Formula bar is displayed

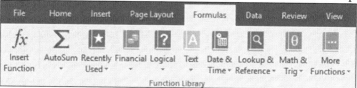

below.

When you enter a formula in a cell, the formula is stored internally and the results are displayed in the cell. You can also view the underlying formula in the formula bar when the cell is active, when you double-click the cell to edit it, or by using the Formulas Tab. In Excel, a formula consists of two elements: operands and calculation operators. Operands identify the values to be used in calculations. An operand can be a constant value, or a variable such as a cell reference, a range of cells, or another formula. A variable refers to a symbol or name that represents something else, which can be a cell address, a range of cells and so on. Calculation operators specify the calculations to be performed. To allow Excel to distinguish formulas from data, all formulas begin with an equal sign (=).

Steps in Entering and Editing Formulas

1. On a new blank workbook, select the cell in which you want to enter the formula

2. Type an equal sign (=) to notify Excel that are imputing the formula.

3. Type the formula's operands and operators.

4. Press Enter to confirm the formula.

Note that you can view many more formulas by clicking on the Show Formulas tab on the Formula tab. However, Excel has three different input modes that determine how it interprets certain key-strokes and mouse actions:

- When you type the equal sign to begin the formula, Excel is prompted into Enter, which is the mode you use to enter texts (such as the formula's operands and operators).

- If you press any keyboard navigation key (such as Page Up, Page Down, or any arrow key) or if you click any other cell in the worksheet, Excel enters Point mode. You can use this mode to select a cell or range as a formula operand. When you're in Point mode, you can use any of the standard range-selection techniques. Excel returns to Enter mode as soon as you type an operator or any character.

- If you press F2, Excel enters Edit mode. You can use this mode to make changes. For example, when you're in Edit mode, you can use the left and right arrow keys to move the cursor to another part of the formula for deleting or inserting characters, and you can also enter the Edit mode by double-clicking the cell or using the formula bar to click anywhere inside the formula text.

The formulas in Excel have been divided into four groups: Arithmetic, Comparison, Text and Reference formulas. Each group of formulas has its own set of operators as discussed below.

Arithmetic Formulas

They are the most commonly used type of formula. They combine numbers, cell addresses, and functions results with mathematical operators to perform calculations. The table below shows some of the arithmetic formulas:

Operator	Name	Example	Results
+	Addition	=10+5	15
-	Subtraction	=10-5	5
-	Negation	=-10	-10
*	Multiplication	=10*5	50
/	Division	=10/5	2
%	Percentage	=10%	0.1
^	Exponentiation	=10^5	100000

The exponentiation operation is a little bit complex. The formula =x^y means that the value x is raised to the power of y.

Comparison Formulas

A comparison formula is used to compare two or more numbers, text strings, cell contents, or function results in the form of a statement. If the statement of comparison is true, the results of comparison is given as the logical value TRUE (which is equivalent to any non-zero value). If the statement is false, the formula returns the logical value FALSE (which is equivalent to zero). Below is a table summarizing comparison operator formulas:

Operator	Name	Example	Results
=	Equal to	=10=5	FALSE
>	Greater than	=10>5	TRUE
<	Less than	=10<5	FALSE
>=	Greater than or equal to	="a">="b"	FALSE
<=	Less than or equal to	="a"<="b"	TRUE
<>	Not equal to	="a"<>"b"	TRUE

Comparison formulas have a variety of uses. For instance, it can be used to determine whether to pay a salesperson a bonus by using a comparison formula to compare actual sales with a predetermined quota. If the sales are greater than the quota, the sales representative is awarded a bonus. It can also be used in monitoring credit collection and can be programmed to send an invoice to a collection agency when a credit is seriously overdue.

Text Formulas

Text formulas are slightly different from arithmetic and comparison formulas as they return texts instead of numerals. Text formulas use the ampersand (&) operator to work with text cells, text strings enclosed in quotation marks, and text function results. One way to use text formulas is to concatenate text strings. For instance, if you enter the formula="soft"&"ware" into a cell, Excel displays software lacking the quotation marks and the ampersand.

Reference Formulas

The reference formulas combine two cell references or ranges to create a single joint reference. The table below summarizes the operators used in reference formulas:

Operator	Name	Description
=(colon)	Range	Produces a range from two cell references e.g. (A1:C5).

(space)	Intersection	Produces a range that is the intersection of two examples e.g. (A1:C5 B2:E8).
, (comma)	Union	Produces a range that is the union of two ranges e.g. (A1:C5, B2; E8).

Controlling Worksheet Calculation using Formulas

As mentioned earlier, the real strength of Excel lies in its capability to perform common and complex calculations through the use of formulas and functions. Excel always calculates a formula when you confirm its entry. The program is designed in such a way that it recalculates existing formulas automatically whenever there is a change in inputted data. However, this feature can be turned off by selecting Formulas, Calculation Options and turning off recalculation or by selecting File, Option and then click Formulas.

Nevertheless, Excel presents you with three calculation options:

- **Automatic** - This is the default calculation mode meaning that Excel recalculates formulas as soon as you enter them and as soon as the data for a formula change.

- **Automatic Except for Data Tables** - In this calculation mode, Excel recalculates all formulas automatically, except for those associated with data tables. This is a good choice if your worksheet includes one or more massive data tables which slows down the recalculation process.

- **Manual** - If you prefer Excel not carrying out automatic calculations, then this mode is best suited for you. You can choose manual calculations in the Excel Options dialog box and turn off recalculation.

If you want to recalculate only one part of your worksheet while manual calculation is on, you can use the steps below:

1. To recalculate a single formula, select the cell containing the formula, click in the Formula bar, and then confirm the cell (by pressing Enter or by clicking on the Enter button).

2. To recalculate a range, select the range, select Home, Find & Select, Replace (or press Ctrl+II), and enter an equal sign (=) in both Find What and Replace with boxes. Click Replace All. Excel "replaces" the equal sign in each formula with another equal sign. This doesn't actually change any formula, but it forces Excel to recalculate each formula.

Cool Tricks

- If you want Excel to recalculate every formula, even those that are unchanged, in all open worksheets, press Ctrl+Alt+Shift+F9.

- Excel supports multi-threaded calculation on computers with either multiple processors or processors with multiple cores. For each processor (or core), Excel sets up a thread (a separate process of execution). Excel can then use each available thread to process multiple calculations concurrently. For a worksheet with multiple, independent formulas, this can dramatically speed up calculations. To make sure the multi-threaded calculation is turned on, select File, Options, click Advanced, and then, in the Formulas section, ensure that the Enable Multi-Threaded Calculation check box is selected.

Copying and Moving Formulas

It may be easy to think of copying and moving ranges that contain formulas the same way regular ranges are copied and moved, but the results are not always accurate or straightforward. To understand how formulas are copied and moved effectively, lets first discuss relative reference format, absolute reference format and mixed-reference format.

Relative Reference Format

When you use a cell reference in a formula, Excel looks at the cell address relative to the location of the formula. For instance, you have the formula =A1*2 in the cell A3. The formula commands Excel to multiply the contents of the cell two rows above this one by 2. This command is called the relative reference format, and it's the default format for Excel. For instance, if you copy this formula to cell A4, the relative reference will still be to multiply the contents of the cell two rows above the highlighted by 2, but the formula will change to =A2*2 because A2 is two rows above A4.

This reference is very useful. Think of this, for instance in your workbook, you just have to copy and paste a certain formula to get your final calculations.

However, the copying and moving of formulas in relative reference format is prone to statistical errors, or rather inaccuracies, when you are not careful as the moved formula may refer to a previous cell instead of increasing cells. This problem is referred to as the problem of relative reference format and arises because Excel assumes that you would want to keep the same cell references on moving a formula. However, this problem can be corrected by absolute reference format as discussed below.

Absolute Reference Format

When you use absolute reference format to refer to a cell in a format, Excel uses the physical address of the cell in undertaking calculations. The dollar sign ($) placed before the row and column of the cell address informs the program to use absolute cell reference when executing a formula. For instance, the formula =$A$1*2 interpreted as the multiplication of the contents of cell A1 by 2. Therefore, no matter where you copy or move this formula, the cell reference doesn't change and it is said to be anchored hence solving the problem of relative reference format.

Mixed-Reference Format

Mixed-Reference format functions similarly to the absolute reference format. In this format, however, you anchor either the cell's row (by placing the dollar sign in front of the row address only - for example, B$6) or its column (by placing the dollar sign in front of the column address only - for example, $B6).

- You can quickly change the reference format of a cell address by using the F4 key. When editing formula, place the cursor to the left of the cell address (or between the row and column values) and then keep pressing F4. Excel cycles through the various formats. When you see the format you want, press Enter. If you want to apply the new reference format to multiple cell addresses, highlight the addresses, press F4 until you get the format you want, and press Enter.

Steps in Copying a Formula Without Adjusting Relative References

You may follow the steps below if you need to copy a formula without changing its relative references:

1. Select the cell that contains the formula you want to copy.

2. Click inside the Formula bar to activate it.

3. Use the mouse or keyboard to select the entire formula.

4. Copy the selected formula.

5. Press **Esc** to deactivate the formula bar.

6. Select the cell in which you want the copy of the formula to appear.

7. Paste the formula.

Additionally, there are two other methods you can use to copy a formula without adjusting its relative cell references:

- To copy a formula from the cell above, select the lower cell and press **CTRL + '**.

- Highlight the formula bar and type an apostrophe (') at the beginning of the formula (it should be to the left of the equal sign) to convert it to text, and then press Enter to confirm the edit, copy the cell, and then paste it in the desired location. Now, delete the apostrophe from both the source and destination cells to convert the text back to formula.

Converting a Formula to a Value

Excel has an option of converting a common overused unchanged formula into a value to speed up the rate of recalculations and free up the worksheet's memory. For example, you may have formulas in part of your worksheet that uses values from a previous fiscal year. Because these numbers aren't likely to change, you can safely convert the formulas into their values. You can use the following steps to convert a formula to a value:

1. Select the cell containing the formula.

2. Double-click the cell or press F2 to activate in-cell editing.

3. Press F9 to change the formula to its value.

4. Press Enter. Excel changes the cell to the value.

Additionally, you may need to replace the results of a formulae in several places. For example, if a formula is in cell C4, you can display its results in other cells by entering =C5 in each of the cells. Excel will update the results of these cells and automatically update them if manual calculations are disabled. You can use these steps to do this:

1. Select the cell containing the formula.

2. Copy the cell.

3. Select the cell or cells to which you want to copy the value.

4. Select Home, display the Paste list, and then select Paste Values. Excel will paste the selected cell's values.

Working with Links in Formulas

How do you work with two workbooks on Excel? For instance, you have data in one workbook that you would want to use in the other workbook. All you need to do is to set up a link between the two workbooks. Excel will automatically update changes in data in one of the worksheets via the link ensuring that you are up-to-date. The workbook that contains the external reference is called the dependent workbook or the client workbook. The workbook that contains the original data is called the source workbook or the server workbook.

External References

A link is usually set up by including an external reference to a cell or range in another workbook. Make sure you are comfortable with the structure of an external reference following the syntax below.

'path[workbookname]sheetname'! reference

path- The drive and directory in which the workbook is located, which can be a local path, a network path, or even an Internet address. You need to include the path only when the workbook is closed.

workbookname- It is the name of the workbook including an extension. Always enclose the workbook name in square brackets ([]). You can omit the workbook name if you are referencing a cell or range in another sheet of the same workbook.

sheetname- It is the name of the worksheet's tab. You can omit the sheetname if the reference is the defined name in the same workbook.

reference- A cell or range reference, or a defined name.

An example of a cell reference would be ='C:\Users\Paul\Documents\ [2017 Budget.xlsx] Details'! $R$7.

Updating Links

A link is useful in avoiding the duplication of formulas and data in multiple worksheets. If one workbook contains the information you might need, you can use a link to reference the data without having to recreate it in another workbook. For a link to be useful however, the data in the dependent workbook should always reflect what actually is in the source workbook. You can update links following the points below:

- Excel automatically updates a link whenever there is a change of data in the source file if both the source and dependent workbooks are open. Additionally, Excel automatically updates the link whenever a source workbook is open when you open the dependent workbook.

- A security warning is displayed by Excel when a source workbook is closed when you open the dependent workbook. The security warnings inform you that automatic updating of links has been disabled and therefore, you need to click on Enable Content to update links.

- You can update a link anytime by choosing Data, Edit Links. An Edit Link dialog box appears, click the link and then click Update Values.

Changing the Link Source

You will need to change the link source to keep the data updated if the name of the source document changes. You can change the link source by editing the external reference directly or change the source by following these steps:

1. With the dependent workbook active, select **DATA**, **EDIT LINKS** to display the Edit Links dialog box.

2. Click the link you want to work with.

3. Click **CHANGE SOURCE**. Excel displays the Change Source dialog box.

4. Find and then select the new source document and then click **OK** to return to the Edit Links dialog box.

5. Click Close to return to the workbook.

Using Cell Ranges in Formulas

Ranges are a group of cells in Excel. The cell groups are either contiguous or non-contiguous. You can name cell ranges, change the size of ranges after you define them, and use named ranges in formulas. The Name Box and the Name Manager help you keep track of named ranges and their cell addresses. You can also use the Paste Names command to create a list of named ranges and their addresses in a worksheet.

Naming a Range

Naming a range is important in the case that you refer to the same cell range over and over. Excel recognizes the name as the cell range and uses the values in those cells to perform a specific function. For example, you have a series of purchase data in a column; instead of referring to them as range C4:C10, you can name the cells PurchaseQ6. Therefore, any time you use the name PurchaseQ6 in a formula, Excel would then use the values in those cells. You can use the following steps to name a given range of cells in your workbook:

1. On a workbook, click Enable Content then proceed to Continue. Click Yes if prompted to make the file a Trusted Document. Click the title of the sheet tab.

2. Select the cells to be named.

3. Click the Name Box located to the left of the Formula bar.

4. Type a name relating to the type of data in the cells. For example, you can type Purchases, and then press Enter. The range name should appear in the Name Box saved.

5. Alternatively, you can use the New Name dialog box and select the cells to be named.

6. Next, on the Formulas tab, in the Defined Names group, click Define Name. The New Name dialog appears.

7. Excel uses the row heading as the range name, shown in the Name text box. However, you have an option of changing the name if you so prefer.

The most common reason for naming a range is to refer to it in formulas and functions. Naming ranges or an individual cell according to the data they contain is a time-saving technique when working with a large amount of data. You can name ranges using three different methods:

- By typing a name in the Name Box next to the formula bar.

- By using the New Name dialog box.

- By using the Create Names from the Selection dialog box.

Rule and guidelines in naming cell ranges include the following:

- The range name should have a maximum of 255 characters in length.

- The range name should have a letter, the underscore character (-), or a backslash (/).

- Range names should not consist solely of short-cuts for selecting columns and rows.

- Range names may not include spaces. The underscore character (-) or period (.) should be used to separate words.

- Range names cannot be the same as a cell reference, such as A7 or$B$3.

A range name should have a certain scope. The scope of a name is the location within which Excel recognizes the name without qualification. Excel requires that the name must be unique within its scope, but you can use the name in different scopes. After creating named ranges, you can select a name in the Name Box drop-down list to select the named range on the worksheet.

Creating a Formula that Operates on a Named Range

You can use the name of any range in a formula by following these steps:

1. Click a cell in your workbook.
2. Type the name of your cell and press **ENTER.**
3. In the adjacent cell to the one you have selected, type a formula e.g. =SUM ().
4. On the Formulas tab, in the Defined Name group, click **USE IN FORMULA.**
5. Select the name of the Formula in the **USE FORMULA** Tab and press **ENTER.**

Chapter Five: Advanced Formulas

In the previous chapter, we discussed using basic formulas and, in this chapter, we are going to discuss using advanced formulas to conditionally summarize data. The formula Tab is illustrated below:

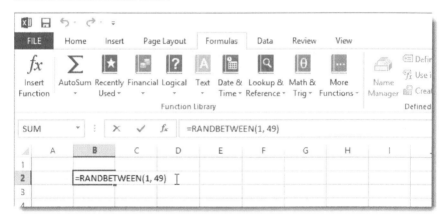

Functions

It is used to apply conditional logic (IF, AND, OR).

Text   Used to modify text.

Lookup &
Reference   Used to create and use named ranges in formulas.

Math &
Trig   It contains SUMIF and SUMIFS.

Using Formulas to Conditionally Summarize Data

Apart from calculations, conditional formulas add another dimension to data analysis by summarizing data that meets one or more criteria. Criteria can be a number, text, or expression that tests which cells to sum, count, or average. A conditional formula used in Excel include the functions SUMIF, COUNTIF, and AVERAGEIF that check for one criterion, or their counterpoints SUMIFS, COUNTIFS, and AVERAGEIFS that check for multiple criteria. All functions used in this chapter are discussed in detail in the next chapter.

SUMIF

The SUMIF function calculates the total of only those cells that meet a given criterion or condition. The syntax for the SUMIF function is SUMIF (Range, Criteria, sum-range). Arguments are values of a function used to perform operations or calculations in a formula. Thus, the arguments of the SUMIF function are Range, Criteria, and sum-range, which, when used together, create a conditional formula in which only those cells that meet a stated Criteria are added. The table below shows the arguments in the SUMIF syntax.

Argument	Explanation
Range	The range of cells that you want the function to evaluate. Also add the matched cells if the Sum-range is blank.
Criteria	The condition or criterion in the form of a number, expression, or text entry that defines the cell to be added.
Sum-range	The cells to add if the corresponding row's cells in the Range match the criteria. If this is blank, use the Range for both cells to add and the cells to evaluate the criteria against.

SUMIFS

The SUMIFS functions adds cells in a range that meet multiple criteria. The order of argument in the SUMIFS function is different from the order used with SUMIF. In a SUMIF formula, the sum-range argument is the third argument as opposed to SUMIFS in which the sum-range argument is the first argument.

COUNTIF

The COUNTIF function counts the number of cells in a given range that meet a specific condition. The syntax for the COUNTIF function is COUNTIF (Range, Criteria). The range is the order of cells to be counted by the formula, and the Criteria are the conditions that must meet the cells to be counted. The condition can be a number, expression, or text entry.

COUNTIFS

The COUNTIFS function counts the number of cells within a range that meet multiple criteria. The syntax is COUNTIFS (Criteria-rangel, Criterial, Criteria-range2, Criteria 2). It is possible to create more than 127 ranges and criteria using the wildcards characters, question mark (?) and asterisk (*) in your criteria.

AVERAGEIF

The AVERAGEIF function is used to return the arithmetic mean of all cells in a range that meet a given criteria. The syntax is similar to SUMIF and is AVERAGEIF (Range, Average-range). In the AVERAGE syntax, Range is the set of cells you want to average. With AVERAGEIF as in the SUMIF formula, the last argument, Average-range, is optional if the range contains the cells that both match the criteria and are used for the average.

Using Formulas to Look Up Data in a Workbook

It may be cumbersome to find specific information in a workbook as it usually contains long and sometimes unspecific data; therefore, you may have to use lookup formulas to find specific data in a workbook. Lookup functions, namely VLOOKUP and HLOOKUP, are an efficient way to search for and insert a value in a cell when the desired value is stored elsewhere in the worksheet or even in a different worksheet or workbook as discussed below.

VLOOKUP

The "V" in VLOOKUP stands for vertical; therefore, this formula is used when the comparison value is in the first column of the table. Excel searches the first column until a match is found and then looks in one of the columns to the right to find the value in the same row. The syntax for the VLOOKUP function is LOOKUP (Lookup-value, Table-array, Col-index-num, Range-lookup). When using VLOOKUP function and arguments, consider the points below:

- An N/A error value is returned when using VLOOKUP if the lookup value is smaller than the smallest value in the first column.

- The Table-array values can be text, numbers, or logical values. Uppercase and lowercase text is equivalent.

- The values in the first column of the Table-array selection must be placed in an ascending sort order: otherwise, VLOOKUP might not give the correct value.

- The fourth argument is the Range-lookup. If the Range-lookup argument is true or omitted, an exact or approximate match is returned. If VLOOKUP cannot find an exact match, it returns the next largest value that is less than the specified value as lookup-value.

- If Range-lookup is false, VLOOKUP finds only an exact match. If an exact match is not found, an error query is returned.

HLOOKUP

The "H" in HLOOKUP stands for horizontal. HLOOKUP searches horizontally for a value in the top row of a table or an array and then returns a value in the same column from a row you specified in the table or array. You can use HLOOKUP when you want to compare values that are located in a row across the top of a data table, or if you want to search a specific row.

Adding Conditional Logic Functions to Formulas

Functions such as AND and OR are used to create conditional formulas resulting in a logical value. Conditional formulas test whether a series or condition evaluate to true or false. Additionally, you can use the IF conditional formula to check if a calculation evaluates as true or false. You can program IF to return one value if the calculation is true or a different value if the calculation is false.

IF

A conditional formula's result is determined by the state of a specific condition or the answer of a logical question. An IF function sets up a conditional statement to test data; therefore, an IF formula returns one value if the specified condition is true and another value if it is false. The IF function requires the following syntax: IF (Logical-test, Value-if-true, Value-if-false).

AND

The AND function returns true if all its argument are true, and false if one or more arguments are false. The syntax is AND (Logical 1, Logical2...). The AND function can be used to determine whether a business meets a strategic goal or whether the sales increased up from the previous year's sales.

OR

As opposed to the AND function where all the arguments have to be true for the function to return a true value, only one of the arguments in the OR function has to be true for the function to return a true value. The OR and AND function share the same syntax. With this function, the arguments must evaluate to logical values such as true or false, or references that contain logical values.

Using Formulas to Modify Text

Data obtained from certain sources, such as people or programs, may have to be modified to match your needs before you can start analyzing it. For instance, you may receive files in a text format with separating data which should be entered into columns or texts with inappropriate capitalization which may not be the format to use in Excel. For this reason, Excel provides you with functions such as PROPER, UPPER, and LOWER functions that you can use to capitalize the first letter in each word of a text string or to convert all characters in a text string to uppercase or lowercase as we are going to discuss below.

Converting Text to Columns

Think of this situation, you have been provided with data relating to alarm systems in homes of an alarm provision company. The information has been coded for the alarm system rather than for use in a spreadsheet. Being an Excel expert, you have been asked to convert the information using Excel to a format that can be analyzed.

In this situation, you will use the Convert Text to Columns Wizard to separate simple cell content, such as first names and last names, into different columns. First, depending on the organization of your data, you can split the cell contents based on a delimiter (divider or separator), such as a space or a comma, or based on a specific column break location within your data. You may follow the steps below:

1. **OPEN** the given data in an Excel workbook and **SAVE** it using an appropriate name.

2. Select the first and last cell i.e. A2:A9. Click the **DATA** tab and then in the Data Tools group, click **TEXT TO COLUMNS**.

3. The Convert Text to Columns Wizard opens with Delimited selected as the default, because Excel recognizes that the data in the selected range is

separated with commas. Click **NEXT** to move to the next step in the wizard.

4. Select **COMMA** as the delimiter. If other delimiters are checked, deselect them.

5. Click **NEXT** and then click **FINISH**. Your data will be separated into columns based on the number of columns.

LEFT

The LEFT function evaluates a string and takes any number of characters on the left side of the string. The format of the function is LEFT (Text, Num-chars). The first string in the Alarm Data workbook containing the employee's phone extension and floor number, which you extract by using the LEFT function.

RIGHT

The RIGHT function is almost identical to the LEFT function, except that the function returns the number of characters on the right side of the text string.

MID

The MID function returns characters in the middle of the spreadsheet as opposed to the RIGHT and LEFT function which return characters on either side of the spreadsheet. Therefore, MID function dictates that your arguments need to include the Text string and then a starting point (Start-num) and numbers of characters (Num-chars).

TRIM

Sometimes in a spreadsheet, there are extra spaces in a cell, either at the end or the beginning of the string or the first and last columns. The TRIM function moves characters at both ends of the string. Text is the only argument; thus, the syntax function is TRIM (Text).

PROPER

The PROPER function capitalizes the first letter in a text string and any other letters in text that follow any character other than a letter. All other letters are converted to lowercase. In the PROPER (Text) syntax, Text can be enclosed in quotation marks, a formula that returns text, or a reference to a cell containing the text you would want to capitalize.

UPPER

The upper function enables you to convert text to uppercase. The syntax is UPPER (Text), with Text referring to the text you want converted to uppercase. The text can be a reference or a text string.

LOWER

As opposed to the UPPER function, the LOWER function converts all uppercase in a text string to lowercase; however, it does not change characters in text that are not letters.

CONCATENATE

The CONCATENATE function can be used to combine text strings together. The syntax for this function is (Text1, Text2, Text3...). You can use the CONCATENATE function to combine the first and last names into two different formats for future mail merges. You do this by typing a comma in a cell and using the cell reference in the CONCATENATE formula.

Chapter 5: FUNCTIONS

Excel provides a number of functions which provide an easy way to work out mathematical operations on a number of cells quickly and conveniently. Functions are prewritten formula which takes a value or values to perform an operation on a range of cells you select and returns a value or values. Functions are used to simplify and shorten formulas on a worksheet, especially those that perform lengthy or complex calculations. Functions can be inserted by following the steps below:

1. Select the cell where you would like the average score to appear.

2. From the Formula tab, choose Insert Function.

3. You can also click on the Function button, found just before the formula bar to use any of Excel's present functions.

4. The Insert Function dialog box appears.

5. Under Select a function, choose from the range of functions available.

6. For instance, choose the SUM function and click OK.

7. The Function Arguments dialog box should appear.

Built-in Functions

Excel provides a variety of built-in functions which can be accessed using the Formula Wizard which can be accessed following the steps below:

1. Click in the cell where you want the result of the formula to be placed. Now click on the = sign in the Formula bar.

2. Click on the drop-down arrow to the left of the Formula bar to select the function you would wish to use.

3. Click on the More Functions Option at the bottom of the list to display a window showing all the available functions.

4. When you have selected the function, the Insert Function dialog box opens to assist you to complete the arguments after the function so that Excel calculates the right result.

5. When each Function is selected, a short description of the function and the type of arguments to be used is displayed in the dialog box.

6. For example, you can use a function such as SUMSQ where you will need to select a range of cells to add together the sums of the squares of the arguments chosen.

7. Click OK when you are sure of the results. The results will then be displayed on the highlighted cell of the spreadsheet. Additionally, you can click on the cell

containing the result, and the formula used will be displayed in the Formula bar.

Note that from the Insert Function dialog box, you can choose All from the list or choose a specific category of functions you are interested in that may contain the function and look for it in there.

Built-In functions can be grouped as follows:

Function Category	Functionality
Mathematical/Trigonometric	It transforms data into a numerical result. Example is the sine and absolute value functions.
Logical	Considers a condition and highlights it as true or false.
Text	Manipulates or creates strings.
Lookup/Reference	Manipulates or examine areas of a worksheet.
Statistical	Return statistical values to sets of numbers, e.g. average, count, min, max etc.

Database	Functions in a similar way to statistical functions; however, datasets are taken from a database.
Date/Time	It performs a calculation on dates, times, and combinations of dates and times.
Engineering	Performs commonly-used engineering calculations relating to Bessel Functions, Complex Numbers or converting between different bases.
Financial	Useful in calculating computations in the financial field, such as interest, monthly, payments, and assist in what-if scenarios.
Information	Used to get information about the contents of a cell.

Mathematical Calculations

Function	Functionality
SUM	Adds its arguments.
SUMIF	Adds the cells specified by one or many given criteria.
SUMPRODUCT	Returns the sums of the products in two arrays.
SUBTOTAL	Returns a subtotal of a filtered list or database.
TRUNC	Truncates a number to an integer.
ROUND	Rounds a number to a specified number of

	digits.
ROUNDUP	Rounds a number up, away from zero.
INT	Rounds a number down to the nearest integer.
ABS	Returns the absolute value of a number.
MOD	Returns the remainder from division.
SQRT	Returns a positive square root.
POWER	Returns the result of a number raised to a power.

SUM

The SUM function totals all the cells in a range, easily and accurately. AutoSum functions in a similar way to the SUM function and even simplifies the task by calculating the total from the adjacent cell up to the first non-numeric cell, using the SUM function in its formula. The SUM function can be used in a number of ways as shown in the table below:

SUM	
SUM (A1, B6, G6)	Will return the sum of the values in cells A1, B6 and G6.
SUM (A1:A23)	Will return the sum of the values in cells A1 to A23.
SUM (A1:A23, F3:F34)	Will return the sum of the values in cells A1 to A23, plus the sum of the values in cells F3 to F34.

SUMIF

The SUMIF function can be used to sum the values in a range that meet the specified criteria. For instance, you want to sum only the values that are larger than 5. You can use the formula: SUMIF (B2:B25,"5"). The syntax for the SUMIF range is SUMIF (range, criteria, [sum-range]). The range is the required range of cells that you want to evaluate by criteria. The cells in each range must be numbers or names, arrays, or references that contain numbers.

Blank and text values are usually ignored by the function the criteria should be in a form of a number, expression, a cell reference, text, or a function that defines which cells will be added. For example, as 45, ">45", B5, "32", the sum range is an optional SYNTAX and it is used to specify the actual cells to add, or if you want to add cells other than those specified in the range argument.

It is important to note that the SUMIF function returns incorrect results when you use it to match strings longer than 255 characters or the strings value.

Cool Trick

- If you want, you can apply the criteria to one range and sum the corresponding values in a different range. For example, the formula =SUMIF (B2:B5," John", C2:C5) sums only the values in the range C2:C5, where the corresponding cells in the range B2:B5 equal "John."

SUMPRODUCT

The SUMPRODUCT function multiplies the corresponding items in the arrays and returns the sum of the results. The SUMPRODUCT can be entered as part of a formula in a cell of a worksheet, and the syntax is SUMPRODUCT (ARRAY1, [ARRAY2...]). This function returns a numeric value; however, it is important to note that if there are non-numeric values in the arrays, they are treated as 0, s by the SUMPRODUCT function.

For instance, you have a series of quantities in cells A1 to A5 and a series of unit prices in B1 to B5. With SUMPRODUCT, you can calculate the total sales with this formula:

=SUMPRODUCT (A1:A5, B1:B5).

SUBTOTAL

This interesting function allows you to count, sum or calculate the average of specified elements of a database. The function requires two arguments:

- The first argument should be a number between 1 and 11 that specifies the operation to be executed: 1 (for AVERAGE); 2 (FOR count); 3 (for COUNTA); 4 (FOR MAX); 6 (for PRODUCT); 7 (for STDEV); 9 (for SUM); 10 (for VAR);

11 (for VARP).

- The second argument is the range covered by the function.

For instance, if you want the sum of B2:45, then you can use this formula =SUBTOTAL (9, B2:B45).

Functions for Rounding up the Decimals

You may program Excel to return only two decimal places; however, Excel will still use the decimal places in the calculations but will only return the 2 decimal places. For instance, in cell A1 you entered 2.2453 and you use a 2-decimal format - you will see 2.25. Then, in cell B1, you write the formula =A1 and make the format "General", and you will still see 2.2453. The roundup functions such as INT, TRUNC, ROUND, ROUNDUP and ROUNDDOWN will eliminate this condition by enabling you to use a specific number of decimals in your calculations. The function is discussed below.

TRUNC

The TRUNC function works in a similar way to INT or ROUNDOWN functions. The TRUNC function removes decimals without rounding. For example, you have 2.2 or 2.7 in cell A1. If you use this formula by typing =(TRUNC) (A1,0), you will get 2. Additionally, if you have 12345 in B1 using a minus sign in the second argument of TRUNC=, (TRUNC B1, -3) WILL RETURN (12,000). This function is useful when you don't want to show the hundreds, the tens and units in a report.

ROUND

The ROUND function removes decimals rounding up the last decimal if the next one is 5 or over. For example, you have 4.126 in cell A1 and use the formula =ROUND (A1,2), so the result will be 4.13.

ABS

The ABS function will remove the negative sign. For instance, if you use the =ABS (A1), 5 will be returned instead of -5 or 5 in a cell.

MOD

The modulo is the remainder left after a division. For example, =MOD (32,6), you will arrive at 2 because you have 5 times 6 is 30 and the remainder is two.

SQRT and POWER

When you want to obtain a square root of a set of data, you use the SQRT function. For example, =SQRT (16) will return 4 because it is the square root of 16 according to mathematical calculations.

Excel lacks a function to extract the cubic root or any other root of a number; however, this can be done by using the POWER function. For example, if you key in =POWER (A1, 2), Excel will return the value of cell A1 raised to 2. Additionally, if you key in:

=POWER (A1, 1/2), you will obtain the square root of the value in cell A1; and

=POWER (A1, 1/3) will obtain the cubic root of the value in cell A1.

Conditional Calculations

Conditional calculations allow you to test cells in a spreadsheet and perform different operations depending on their content as discussed below.

IF () Function

The IF function returns one value if the condition is true, or another value if the condition is false. The IF function can be entered as part of a formula in a cell of a worksheet. The syntax for the IF function is (condition, [value-if-true-], [value-if-false]). The condition is the value that you want to test. The value-if-true is the value that is returned if conditional evaluates to true. Value-if-false is the value that is returned if conditional evaluates to false. The IF function can be combined with other functions, such as AND, OR etc. as discussed below.

AND Function

The AND function, when combined with the IF function, allows you to test for multiple conditions. When using the AND function, all conditions within the AND function must be true for the condition to be met. Look at the examples below:

IF (AND (A2=" Anderson", B2>80), 'MVP", "regular") returns "MVP"; and

IF (AND (B2>=80, B2<=100), "Great Score", "Not Bad") returns "Great Score"; and

IF (AND (A2=" Anderson", A3=" Smith", A4=" Johnson"), 100,50) returns 100.

OR FUNCTION

The IF function, when combined with the OR function, allows you to test for multiple conditions; however, only one or more of the conditions within the OR function needs to be true for the condition to be met. Check out the examples below:

=IF (OR (A2=" Apples", A2=" Oranges"), "Fruit", "Other") returns "Fruit".

IF (OR (A4=" Bananas", B4. =100), 999, "N/A") RETURNS 999.

Cutting up & Piecing Together Text Strings Using Text functions

Function	Functionality
CONCATENATE	Joins together two or more text strings =CONCATENATE (A2, B2).
LEFT	Returns a specified number of characters from the start of a supplied text string =LEFT(C2,8).
MID	Returns a specified number of characters from the middle of a supplied text string

	=MID(A2,2,2).
RIGHT	Returns a specified number of characters from the end of a supplied text string =RIGHT (A2,3).
REPT	Returns a string consisting of a supplied text string, repeated a specified number of times =REPT(A2,3).
LEN	Returns the length of a supplied text string =LEN(A2).
EXACT	Tests if two supplied text strings are exactly the same and if so, returns true; otherwise, returns false. =EXACT (A2, F2).
MATCH	Returns the relative position of an item in an array that matches the specified value in a specified order. =MATCH (D2, $D$2: D2,0).

VLOOKUP FUNCTION

The VLOOKUP (vertical lookup) function is used to find specific information in a spreadsheet. It can also be used to return a worksheet in to return a value from a table located either in the same sheet, another sheet or another workbook which is related to the given value. Say you have a parts list in a table on one sheet containing thousands of parts numbers and their related information. The table shows the part number in the first column, the part description in the second column, the parts supplier in the third column, the parts price in the fourth column and so on. On a separate sheet, you have an invoice with columns for the Quantity, the Part number, the part Description, the Price and the Total. When you enter the part number in the Part number column of the Invoice, the VLOOKUP function is used to get the details for the Description column and the Unit Price column for the part number. Although the IF () function can be very useful in these circumstances, it is limited to either true or false outcomes but, in these types of examples with large inventories or contact list, we need a function that can handle multiple outcomes. The VLOOKUP () function is ideally suited for this sort of calculation.

The VLOOKUP function is (lookup value, lookup table range, value column). The lookup value is the value you wish to look for in the table. The lookup table range is the range on the worksheet that contains the lookup table. You can use a reference to a range or a range name. The values in the first column of the table are the values searched by lookup-value. These values can be text, numbers, or logical values. The third argument, the value column indicates which column of the table is to be used for the actual result. The range-lookup argument specifies whether you want

VLOOKUP to find an exact match, or an approximate match.

Pivot Tables

Excel provides you with the pivot table which are useful to summarize, analyze, explore and present data with ease. PivotTables are designed for:

1. Querying large amounts of data.

2. Sub-totaling and aggregating numeric data, i.e. summarizing data by categories and subcategories, and creating custom calculations and formulas.

3. Expanding and collapsing levels of data to focus your results and drilling down to details from the summary data for areas of interest to you.

4. Transposing data-moving rows to columns or columns to rows (or "pivoting") to see different summaries of the source data.

5. Filtering, sorting, grouping and conditionally formatting the most useful and interesting subset of data to enable you to focus on the information that you want, without having to write any formulas.

6. Presenting concise, attractive, and annotated or printed reports.

Steps in Creating a Pivot Table

First, you should ensure you have a worksheet which is usually the source data for the pivot table, and then follow the steps below:

1. Select the range of cells that contains the data, along with column headings.

2. On the **INSERT TAB**, in the Tables group, click **PIVOTTABLE.**

3. The **CREATE PIVOTTABLE** dialog box opens.

4. Under **CHOOSE THE DATA YOU WANT TO ANALYZE**, ensure that **SELECT A TABLE OR RANGE** is selected, and then in the **TABLE/RANGE** box, make sure the range of cells that you want to use are listed.

5. Under **CHOOSE WHERE YOU WANT THE PIVOTTABLE REPORTS TO BE PLACED**, choose either the **NEW WORKSHEET** or **EXISTING WORKSHEET** and click **OK.**

6. An empty PivotTable report is added on the specified worksheet, along with the PivotTable Field List from which you can select the fields that you would like to add to create a layout and customize the PivotTable report.

7. To place any field in the default area of the layout section, **SELECT THE CHECK BOX** next to the field name in the field section. By default, nonnumeric fields are added to the Row Labels area, numeric fields are added to the values areas, while date/time hierarchies are added to the Column Labels area.

8. To place a field in a specific area of the layout section, you can also right-click the field name in the field section, and then select **ADD TO REPORT FILTER**, **ADD TO COLUMN LABEL**, **ADD TO ROW LABEL**, or **ADD TO VALUES**.

9. You can also drag a field to the area that you want by clicking and holding the field name in the field section, and then dragging it to an area in the layout section.

Statistical Functions

Excel offers a wide range of in-built statistical functions used to solve mathematical problems; for instance, the slope and y-intercept of a line, the standard deviation of a data sample, and the mean, median, mode of a set of values. Here are some of the basic statistical functions:

FUNCTION	FUNCTIONALITY
AVERAGE (range)	Returns the average of its arguments.
AVERAGEA (range)	Returns the average of its arguments, including numbers, text, and logical values.
MEDIAN (range)	Returns the number in the middle of a range of data.

MODE (range)	Returns the most frequently occurring or repetitive value in a range of data.
COUNT (range)	Counts how many numbers are in a range of data.
COUNTA (range	Counts how many values are in a range of data.
MAX (range)	Returns the maximum value of a range.
MIN (range)	Returns the minimum value of a range.
LARGE (range, n)	Returns the k – the largest value in a data set.
SMALL (range, n)	Returns the k – the smallest value in a data set.

AVERAGE and AVERAGEA

The AVERAGEA function returns the average of a group of supplied values. Unlike AVERAGE, AVERAGEA will also evaluate the logical values true and false, and the numbers represents as text, whereas AVERAGE just skips these values during calculation. The syntax for the AVERAGEA function is AVERAGEA (value 1, [value2] ...). Value 1 is a value or reference to a value that can be evaluated as a number, while value2 is a value or reference to a value that can be evaluated as a number.

The AVERAGE function returns the average of values supplied as multiple arguments. The AVERAGE function handles up to 255 individual arguments, which can include numbers, cell references, ranges arrays and constants.

COUNT and COUNTA

If you want to count the number of cells that are not blank, COUNT and COUNTA will return a different result if in one of the cells there is a text or a space.

=COUNT (B2:B7) will return 6 if only numbers are present in cells B2to B7and 5 if there is a letter, an empty cell OR A SPACE in one of the cells.

=COUNTA (B2:B7) will return 6 unless one of the cells is empty. If all the cells contain numbers, letters OR SPACES, the result will be 6.

LARGE and SMALL

The MAX and MIN functions would give the largest and smallest value from a list of values but, what if you want the second or third largest value or the second smallest value, use LARGE and SMALL functions as follows:

=LARGE (A1:A5,2), =LARGE (A1:A5,3), =SMALL (A1:A5,2).

As a matter of fact, you can also get the MIN and MAX values using these functions.

=LARGE (A1:A5,1), =SMALL (A1:A5,1).

Linear Regression Functions

Excel has some in-built functions that allow you to perform statistical computations, such as determining the slope of a graph, y-intercept, correlation coefficient, and R-squared values of a set of data. Linear regression functions, such as SLOPE (), INTERCEPT (), AND CORREL () are easier and faster to compute than plotting the data; however, a visual graph shows trends in the data better than any other tool. The table below shows statistical data and their functions:

Function	Functionality
SLOPE	The SLOPE function returns the slope of the regression line through the given data points. =SLOPE (Y CELL RANGE, X CELL RANGE).

INTERCEPT	It calculates the point at which a line will intersect the y-axis using a best-fit regression line plotted through the known x values and y values. =INTERCEPT (Y CELL RANG, X CELL RANGE). =INTERCEPT (C2:C6, A2:A6).
CORREL	Returns the correlation coefficient between two data sets =CORREL (Y cell range cell range.

STEDV

For error analysis, we use the STDEV function. When we carry out a number of repetitive measurements of one quantity, we find the average value. This does not, however, tell us anything of the precision of our measurement. The standard deviation of the measured values will give a measure of the precision. To quickly determine the standard deviation of any measurement, use Excel's built-in STDEV () function.

= STDEV (A2:A6)

Statistical Analysis

Excel has some added in-built features which support statistical analysis; however, statistical data analysis in Excel is not recommended for analyzing dataset with a large sample size or a large number of variables performing advanced statistical analyses, or for projects in which a number of procedures need to be performed. Excel is perfect for basic analysis of data, but using it for statistical analysis can be disadvantageous due to the following reasons:

- Missing values are handled inconsistently, and sometimes incorrectly.

- Data has to be organized differently according to the analysis you wish to perform.

- Most analyses can only be done on one column at a time. This makes it inconvenient to do the same analysis on many columns.

- There is no log or record of how an analysis was accomplished.

- It lacks important features for advanced analyses.

Analysis ToolPak

The Analysis ToolPak must be loaded to access tools which are useful in generating descriptive statistics and histograms of grade distributions. First, check to see if the Data Analysis command is available in the Analysis group on the Data tab. If the Data

Analysis menu is available, then it indicates that the Analysis ToolPak is already loaded. If not, follow the steps below:

1. Choose **ADDS-INS** from the Excel Option found through the Microsoft Office Button.

2. In the **MANAGE** drop-down menu, select Excel **ADD-INS** and click **GO**.

3. In the **ADD-INS AVAILABLE** box, select the **ANALYSIS TOOLPAK** check box, and then click **OK**.

4. If you get prompted that the Analysis ToolPak is not currently installed on your computer, click **YES** to install it.

5. A configuration progress screen for Microsoft Office appears and, once completed, the Data Analysis menu should appear on the **DATA** menu in the **ANALYSIS** group.

Descriptive Statistics

Descriptive statistics offers the quickest way to get mean and standard deviation for an entire group of values using the Data Analysis tools. This generates simple descriptive statistics like average, median and standard deviation for a collection of data. You can choose several adjacent columns for the input Range and each column is analyzed separately. The labels in the first row are used to label the output, and the empty cells are ignored. If there are more than adjacent columns to be analyzed, then one has to repeat the process for each group of adjacent columns. Follow the steps below to generate these statistics:

1. From the **DATA MENU** in the **ANALYSIS** group, select **DATA ANALYSIS.**

2. The **DATA ANALYSIS** dialog box opens.

3. In the **DATA ANALYSIS DIALOG BOX**, choose **DESCRIPTIVE STATISTICS.**

4. In the **DESCRIPTIVE STATISTICS** dialog box, specify the cells that contain your data in the Input Range box. Select the **SUMMARY STATISTICS** checkbox in the lower left corner.

5. By default, statistics is generated on a new worksheet. If you want the statistics to appear on the same worksheet, click the **OUTPUT RANGE** button and specify a destination cell for the statistics. You can also specify a name for the new worksheet.

Conclusion

In this book, we have delved deeper into Excel formulas and functions. We have discussed that formulas and functions are really the features that give Excel the power and capability to carry out statistical computations expediting time it takes to perform manual analyses and coming up with outputs that are more dynamic and engaging to users. Both formulas and functions need to be written in a specific way, referred to as a syntax in order to calculate properly. Additionally, both functions and formulas require at least one argument, which, on the most basic level, identifies the values for which perform the action.

While Excel offers hundreds of functions and categorizes them based on their functionality, this book covers only a small portion of formulas and functions plus their tricks, which are important in common statistical calculations. We hope this book has been key in you learning about Excel formulas and functions. Always remember that practice makes perfect. Thank you.

Made in the USA
San Bernardino, CA
24 September 2018